GERALD F. FISCHBACH AND ROBERT S. FROST

A comprehensive, friendly, and effective course of study for the development of vibrato on violin, viola, cello, and string bass in private or group instruction.

Dear String Student:

Vibrato is the frosting on our tonal cake. It sweetens the flavor of our sound, and makes it more interesting, more colorful, more complex. Vibrato also adds intensity to our sound. As a tool for strengthening our emotional message, it helps us to laugh and to weep, to sing of love, and to shout in anger.

A well-balanced vibrato can actually make playing feel easier, by helping the left hand and arm to stay well aligned and balanced. Vibrato can also play an important supporting role in connecting notes, when you learn to "pour" your vibrato from one note to the next without stopping it.

And not least important, vibrato is a badge of tonal maturity.

Enjoy your journey to mastery. **Viva Vibrato!**

Gerald Fischbach
Gerald Fischbach

Robert S. Frost
Robert S. Frost

Instrumentation

Violin   Viola   Cello   String Bass
Piano Accompaniment   Teacher's Manual & Score

ISBN 0-8497-3371-5

kjos Neil A. Kjos Music Company • San Diego, California

I. VIBRATO READINESS

Vibrato is a balanced, rocking movement. It is much like waving hello, knocking on a door, salting your food, or patting dog. When you are balanced, the vibrato rocks easily; vibrato "just happens." When you are out of balance, muscles tighten, parts of you squeeze and pinch, and vibrato is difficult.

Before we actually begin vibrato exercises, let's run through a Vibrato Readiness Checklist.

Vibrato Readiness Checklist

☑ **Body.** Does your body swing easily backward and forward, from left to right, and around in small circles? Of course it does! You've been an expert at those motions since long before you learned to play. Try these gentle movements and notic how easily you move.

Now place your instrument in playing position. Again, move left to right, back and forward, and in small circles. Are you still moving as easily? If so, good; you have successfully included your instrument into your balanced body system. If not, ask your teacher if you are holding (balancing) your instrument correctly.

☑ **Arm.** Put your left hand in playing position. Does your elbow swing freely? If not, you are tense in the shoulder, and you may also be squeezing the neck of your instrument with your hand. Reach over and hold the violin up with your right hand. Can you now release some left arm tension that perhaps you didn't even know you had? Swing your left elbow again.

Now it's time for our first **Swingercise!**

 #1: SWINGPLOP

Photo #1

1. With your instrument in playing position, use your right hand to hold it steady and secure. Let your left arm hang by your side. Now swing your left arm in a lazy arc, forward and backward.
2. After a few lazy swings, use a forward *swing* to toss the hand up to the neck, then drop the arm so that the fingers *plop* on the fingerboard. Let the fingers "spring" a little on the fingerboard. See *Photo #1*.
3. Do Swingplop three to five times.

Photo #2

☑ **Hand.** In playing position, does your hand balance easily on the end of your forearm? Does it move freely from the wrist? Check the line from fingers through hand and forearm to elbow: there should be no unusual bends or kinks. See *Photo #2*.

Photo #3

☑ **Thumb and Fingers**. No squeezing allowed! Tap your thumb. It should be flexible, touching the violin neck with the inside edge, not the center, of the thumb pad. See *Photo #3*.

Tap your fingers. They should bounce and float, touching the string on the fleshy pad a little behind the fingernail, where delicious tone is found, not near the nail, where you may produce a more pinched sound.

Contact should be made with just the thumb and finger pad; if anything else is touching continuously in one spot, your vibrato will get stuck. You can feel a light brushing of the neck with the base of your first finger, but take care not to pinch the neck like a lobster claw!

Photo #4

 **#2: HAPPYTAPPY**

1. Tap your thumb again. Tap, tap, tap! Now tap your third finger. Tap, taptap, tap! And again the thumb.
2. Now third and fourth together. Then thumb. Now fourth alone. And (guess what?) thumb.
3. Next, middle fingers together, then thumb. Then second alone, and thumb.
4. Now first and second, followed by thumb. And first alone, then thumb.
5. Now mix them up some more, switching regularly between fingers and thumb. See *Photo #4*.

 **#3: SHAKE, RATTLE, AND ROLL**

Photo #5

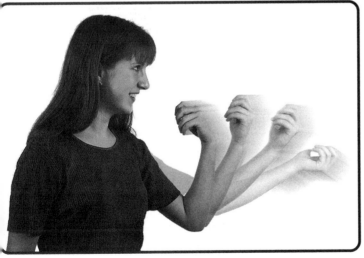

1. Without your instrument, hold in your left hand a (real or imaginary) matchbox half-filled with rice kernels.
2. Now with your left hand, knock on an imaginary door in front of you. As you shake and rattle, roll your arm around to simulate cello or bass playing position.
3. Roll your hand and arm around some more, to play vibrato on your "air" violin. See *Photo #5*.

Extra tip: it can be fun and instructive to do *Swingercise* #3 with both hands, mirroring the actions of the left hand with the right.

☑ With our Vibrato Readiness Checklist in good order, it's time to move on to actual vibrato exercises, and to give birth to a beautiful new **vibrato!**

II. THE BIRTH OF A VIBRATO

A selection of the exercises in this section should be repeated every day, even two or three times through the course of a day, until your vibrato is born, and for a while thereafter. Some will be more useful to you than others; your teacher will help you decide from week to week which combination of exercises is best for you. You will probably be doing these exercises for several weeks to several months. Vibrato comes sooner to some than to others, but everyone gets it eventually.

You should do these exercises during your regular daily practice sessions, of course. Additionally, some of them are good "TV Games"—they can be done while doing other things, such as reading or even watching television! The more often you practice these movements each day, the sooner your vibrato will come.

 **#4: PALMPATS**

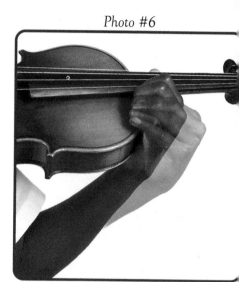
Photo #6

1. With your instrument in playing position, place the palm of your left hand on the instrument's rib, on the E-string side. Allow your fingers to fall naturally onto the top of the instrument. Notice how nicely curved the fingers are.
2. Now with the palm of your left hand, pat the rib. Patpatpat! Let your fingers wiggle from loose knuckles (especially the one nearest the fingernail), so that the fingertips rock in one spot. See *Photo #6*.
3. You can do Palmpats with all four fingers down, or just one or two. Try out all the possibilities you can think of!
4. Palmpat Rhythms. Pat the following rhythm patterns 10 times each:

 **#5: TOPTAPS**

Photo #7

1. Put your instrument in playing position, and use your right hand to hold it steady and secure.
2. With your left thumb tucked under the neck as in a high position, swing your hand over the fingerboard and tap the top of the instrument, on the G-string side.
   • For right now, just to get the "swing" of it, tap at moderate, comfortable speed, in no particular rhythm.
   • Your hand and fingers should be very loose and floppy, with curved, springy fingers. See *Photo #7*.

3. Name rhythms. Tap "Jiminy Cricket! Jiminy Cricket!"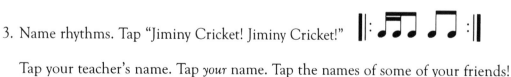

Tap your teacher's name. Tap *your* name. Tap the names of some of your friends!

Write the rhythm of your teacher's name here: _____

Write the rhythm of your name: _____

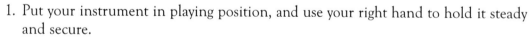

Photo #8

4. Toptap Rhythms. To the following rhythms, tap the top of the instrument as in Step 2. During the rest, swing your hand in an arc back to first position, and your elbow out to the left, as a kind of "windup" to the next Toptap. Stay above the fingerboard with the fingers. Pivot on the thumb, which stays in place. See *Photo #8.*

Tap the following rhythm patterns 10 times each (♩ = 60):

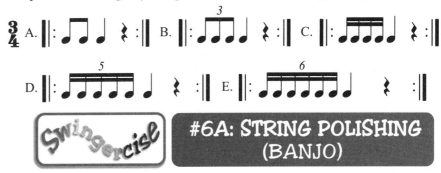

#6A: STRING POLISHING (BANJO)

1. Hold your violin like a banjo, cradled in your right arm, the scroll about as high as your nose.
2. With your left hand in playing position, polish a string with one of your middle fingers. Swing the whole arm.
   • Polish most of the string, from first position to near the end of the fingerboard.
   • Slide on the fleshy finger pad, a little to the thumb side of center.
   • Slide light as a feather.
   • When you change directions, the finger should flex a little, especially from the nail joint.
   • Notice that the thumb is also polishing the neck, and the base of the first finger gently polishes the side of the fingerboard. See *Photo #9a.*
3. Now gradually make the polishing motion smaller and smaller, and a little faster.
4. Eventually, the finger pad stays in one place, somewhere around third or fourth position. The thumb and base of the first finger are still polishing.
5. Now anchor the thumb, opposite the 1st finger. The base of the 1st finger still polishes the side of the neck.
6. Repeat steps 2–5 five times.

Photo #9a

#6B: STRING POLISHING (SHOTGUN RIGHT)

Hold your violin on your right shoulder, like a shotgun. See *Photo #9b.* In this posture, repeat the above steps 2–5 five times.

Photo #9b

#6C: STRING POLISHING (SHOTGUN LEFT)

Move the "shotgun" to the "wrong" (left) shoulder. Note that your left elbow should be as high as the back of your violin. See *Photo #9c.* Repeat steps 2–5 five times again.

#6D: STRING POLISHING (CONTRACTING WOBBLE)

Finally, transform the "shotgun" into a violin: swing your elbow under the instrument, tilting it to normal playing position. Once more, repeat steps 2–5 five times.

Photo #9c

#7: THE WAVE

Photo #10

1. With your instrument in playing position, bring your left hand up to about fourth position. Open the hand so that the palm is facing you. Now wave to yourself!
2. Pick up your bow. Play long, slow strokes on the A string. Wave to yourself again. Listen to your pretty vibrato! See *Photo #10*.
3. Play your Wave Vibrato on other strings.
4. Play *Wave Duet* using your Wave Vibrato on Part A, which should be played entirely using open strings. Play Part B using smooth string crossing waves.

1. Wave Duet ♩ = 96

Hermann Op. 20, no. 2

Photo #11

 **#8: 'TWEENTAPS**

1. *'Tweentaps* is just like *Toptaps* (*Swingercise #5*), except it is performed on the fingerboard, in a high position, *in between* your E and A strings.
2. Go through the Toptap Rhythms again, 10 times each. (See page 5.)
3. Use your second or third finger.
4. Be sure your wrist and finger joints stay springy and flexible.
5. Do aim for the space in between strings; if you tap on a string instead, you may find your fingers and wrist getting stiff. See *Photo #11*.

Photo #12

 **#9: HANDSHINE**

1. With the palm of your right hand facing you, place the tip of your left thumb in your right palm. Now embrace your left thumb loosely in your right fist.
2. With a waving motion of the left hand and arm, use your middle fingers to gently polish the back of your right hand and wrist. See *Photo #12*.
   - Feel the left hand swinging from the bottom of the thumb, way down near the wrist.
   - There should be free movement from all joints of the finger, thumb, and wrist.
3. Gradually narrow the motion so that the second or third finger pad settles into one spot.

Photo #13

 **#10: STRINGSHINE**

Now we will move *Handshine* to the violin. With your thumb in third position, polish the A string as in steps 2–3 of *Swingercise #9*. See *Photo #13*.

Let's Rap!

2. Rap Music

1. Play the following "Rap Tune" to *Swingercise #8, 9, or 10*.

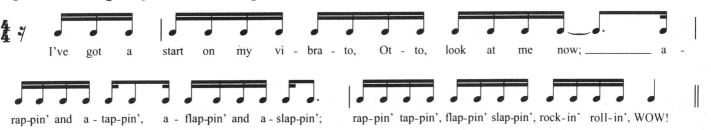

I've got a start on my vi-bra-to, Ot-to, look at me now;_____ a-

rap-pin' and a-tap-pin', a-flap-pin' and a-slap-pin'; rap-pin' tap-pin', flap-pin' slap-pin', rock-in' roll-in', WOW!

2. Make up and tap out your own Rap Tunes!

#11: STICKYTAPS

Stickytaps is just like '*Tweentaps*, with one important difference: magic super glue!

1. Put a drop of this (pretend) magic super glue on your third finger pad.
2. Now start '*Tweentaps*, using the Toptap Rhythms. ♩ = 60. Tap the following rhythm patterns 10 times each:

3. Here's the magic part:
   - On the first tapping of each rhythm, the super glue has no effect—tap as usual.
   - On the second, the glue works instantly, and you continue the tapping motion with your finger stuck to the fingerboard. Notice how flexible your finger and wrist joints are.
   - On the rest before the third tapping, the super glue magically lets go, so that you tap again as usual.
   - Continue through the 10 repetitions with the odd-numbered repetitions "unglued," and the even-numbered ones "glued."

Now let's take your "magic super glue" vibrato on a ride to one of the moons of Jupiter!

3. Sunrise on Ganymede

Fischbach-Frost

4. Merry Maiden Waltz

Lehár

You may find that by now you have a functional, if young, vibrato started. Do the next two *Swingercises* if you need just a little more help. They are also useful as an alternative to one or more of the previous *Swingercises*; your teacher will guide you through the best pathway to success for you.

#12: THE WAWA

Some electric guitar amplifiers have a "wawa" circuit—a sort of wild electronic vibrato whose speed the player manipulates via a pedal. It works like a car's gas pedal: the more you push it, the faster it goes. The following exercises, which work a little like a wawa pedal pushed to various speeds, are to be played with a metronome, first without, then with the bow.

1. Put your instrument in playing position, and use your right hand to hold it steady and secure.
2. With the heel of your left hand leaning against the violin's rib and your hand and thumb in third position, place your 2nd finger on E on the A string. Now do a "Wawa": rock your finger forward and back. The forward-back cycle should feel like one action with a rebound. Do several more in a row, at a tempo that is comfortable for you.

   You and your teacher may find it is better for you to do the Wawa with a backwards action and a forward rebound. Eventually, we don't pay attention to whether the motion starts forward or backward.

3. Wawa with your 3rd finger, F# on the A string.

In example (a) the higher notehead represents the vibrato impulse, and the lower notehead is the passive rebound. Thus, there are two vibrato impulses per measure, one per 8th-note beat (eight in ex. b).

4. Do the above with your first finger (D on the A string), then your fourth (G on the A string).

#13: WEEKLY WAWA

Now we will take our Wawa through a metronome acceleration trip that will lead us to vibrato's doorstep in three weeks!

Week I: Record your progress using the **Metronome Acceleration Checklist** found on the inside back cover. On each day of Week I, play the following exercise and song four times at each of the settings indicated for that day. Note that each day starts and ends two markings faster than the previous day.

5. Waawaa ♪ = 80 – 155 or 80 – 152

Play this finger pattern on all four strings.

6. Painting a Rainbow ♪ = 80 – 155   Wohlfahrt Op. 38, no. 47

Play this piece using separate bows and also observing the dashed slurs.

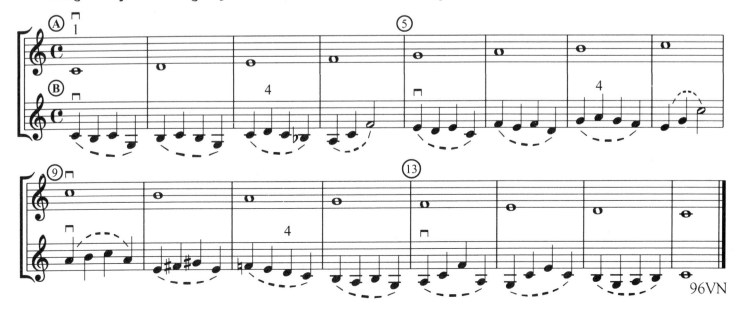

96VN

Week II: To the following exercise and songs, continue the Week I plan. (See **Metronome Acceleration Checklist** on the inside back cover.) Notice that we are continuing with the metronome clicking half as frequently. There are now two complete vibrato cycles per click.

7. Wawawawa ♩ = 70 – 145 or 72 – 132

Play this finger pattern on all four strings.

8. Ring Out the Old (Two-Part Round)

French

The asterisk ✳ indicates the time for the second entrance of the melody.

9. Jacob's Ladder

Spiritual

Play this piece starting down bow (⊓) as well as up bow (∨) for further development of your vibrato.

10. Squid Dreams

Hohmann Bk. 1, no. 49

Play this piece using separate bows and also observing the dashed slurs.

11. Sven's Snowshoes

Norwegian Folk Song

Week III: To the following exercise and songs, continue the weekly plan as before, but advance the speed range only one notch from day to day. Again, see the inside back cover for the **Metronome Acceleration Checklist.**

12. wwwWWOW! ♩ = 135 – 180 or 120 – 180

Play this finger pattern on all four strings.

13. Yorkshire Pudding

English Folk Song

Play this melody using separate bows and also observing the dashed slurs.

14. Moldau Mood (Round)

Bohemian Folk Song

The asterisk ✳ indicates the second entrance of the melody.

15. Sluggo the Singing Snail

Hohmann Bk. I, no. 91

Remember: snails sing slowly!

16. Sad Sam's Serious Song

Wohlfahrt Op. 38, no. 41

III. THE DEVELOPING VIBRATO

The following tunes and exercises are fun to play, and they help your newborn vibrato become mature in several important ways.

17. Go Tell Aunt Rhody

Traditional

This is surely the saddest song ever written in a major key! Use your widest, wobbliest, *saddest* vibrato!

18. Wauwatosa Wawa

Wohlfahrt Op. 38, no. 34

Play this piece using separate bows and also observing the dashed slurs.

19. Pierre's Stairs   ♩ = 100 – 112

French Folk Song

20. Happy New Year (Round)   ♩ = 88 - 96

Swiss

21. Dreams of Love ♩ = 88 - 100

Liszt

22. La Folia ♩ = 69 – 72

Corelli

23. Gold and Silver Waltz ♩ = 132 – 144

Lehár

A new vibrato that works well in 3rd position sometimes is confused at first in the lower positions. "Play" Song #24 *Sigh!* first without the bow. From measure 2, place one, two, or three right hand fingers between the heel of your left hand and the violin rib. Your right fingers will serve as a temporary "rib extension," providing support for the left arm. When the vibrato is swinging smoothly, take away your right fingers. Put them back if the vibrato gets confused again.

24. Sigh!

25. Pierrot's Basement Door   ♩ = 76   French Folk Song

Slowly play the first phrase of *Pierrot's Basement Door* (A). Create a wide, easy vibrato on each note. In the fermata measures, move your hand back a half step, and play *Pierrot* again, using the indicated pitches written in versions B, C, D, E.

26. Cellar Stairs   ♩ = 76   French Folk Song

Play this piece using separate bows and also observing the dashed slurs.

27. Where is John? (Round)   ♩ = 92 – 100   Smetana

The asterisk * indicates the second entrance of the melody.

28. Blue Bells of Scotland ♩ = 84

Scottish Folk Song

29. Southern Roses ♩ = 104

Strauss

Play this piece in both the A string and G string registers, using separate bows and also observing the dashed slurs.

30. Manta Ray Ballet ♩ = 84

Wohlfahrt Op. 45, no. 8

31. Midnight Special Blues ♩ = 104

Unknown

IV. THE MATURING VIBRATO

In this section, your vibrato will develop agility, quick starts, and the ability to move through slurs and shifts.

 **#15: VIBRATO BURSTS**

These variations on a one-octave scale are intended to give your vibrato a quick start and to speed up a sluggish vibrato. Each day, choose a different key and different position. In variation A, lift fingers slightly during the rests or in between quarter notes (♪ ❼ and ♩ mean the same thing here). In Variations B through D, "zap" the vibrato on the accents. ♩ = 60–80 for all variations.

32. Star Bursts
Folk Song

Play *Star Bursts* using variations A through D from *Swingercise #15.*

33. Duke Bursts Repetizione ad nauseum ♩ = 88
arr. Fischbach-Frost

34. John Peel ♩ = 116
English Folk Song

35. Vivaldi Goes Ballistic! ♩ = 66
Vivaldi

Accent vigorously with the vibrato and the bow.

36. Wiggwobb Waltz

Fischbach-Frost

Play *Wiggwobb Waltz* in various octaves, positions, and keys. For every two slurred notes, have just one continuous vibrato.

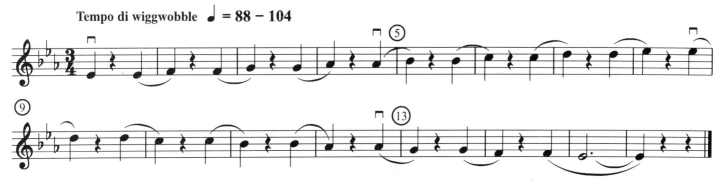

37. Graceful Skaters Waltz ♩ = 104 – 116

Fischbach-Frost

Imagine a graceful skater moving from foot to foot on every downbeat, weight and balance shifting smoothly. With your vibrato, do the same from finger to finger. Pour the vibrato from one finger to the next, so that it doesn't stop between notes.

38. Long, Long, Ago ♩ = 84

Bayley

Keep the vibrato alive through the slurs.

39. All Through the Night ♩ = 96

Welsh Folk Song

#17: THE SHIGGLE

40. Shiggle, Shiggle ♩ = 56 – 60

Anderson-Frost

Keep the feeling of vibrato going through the shift. Finger pressure should be as light as possible, especially during the shiggle (shift/wiggle).

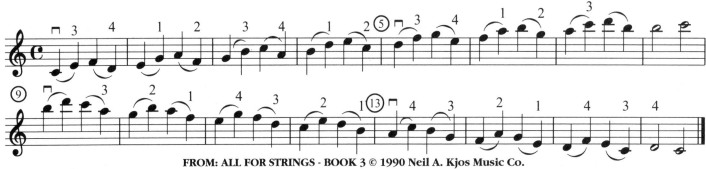

FROM: ALL FOR STRINGS - BOOK 3 © 1990 Neil A. Kjos Music Co.

41. Slippery Sal Slides Softly ♪ = 72

Fiorillo

42. Paco's Bell ♪ = 76

Pachelbel

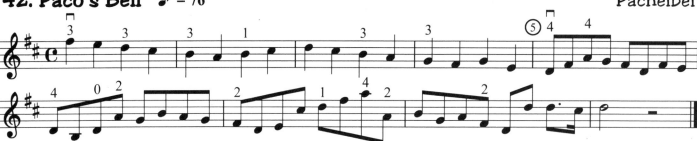

43. Going Home ♩ = 76

Dvořák

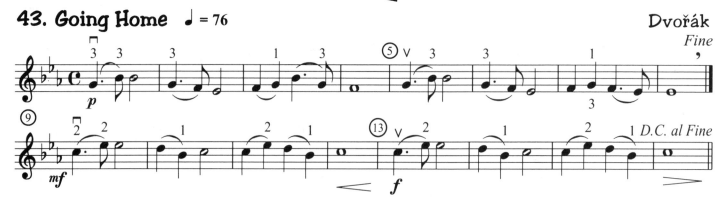

44. To a Wild Rose ♩ = 58

MacDowell

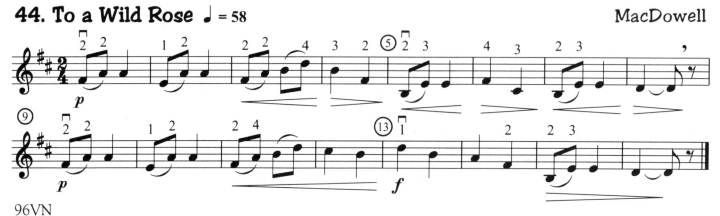

45. Melody ♩ = 76 — Rubinstein

46. Londonderry Air ♩ = 56 — Irish Folk Song

47. Blessed Spirits ♩ = 76 — Gluck

48. Still, Still, Still ♩ = 80 — Traditional German

96VN

V. THE ARTISTIC VIBRATO

In Part V, you will increase your expressive control, and learn to think artistically in your use of vibrato.

#18: VIBRATO SWELLS

To various one-octave scales, start measure 1 with almost no vibrato; increase vibrato intensity to maximum at the beginning of measure 2; decrease to measure 3; etc. Use the following meters and note values. Try each variation starting up bow (V) as well as down bow (⊓) for further development of your vibrato and tone. ♩ = 60 for all variations.

#19: SPEEDWIDTHERY

To various one-octave scales, manipulate the vibrato width and speed as indicated. Try each variation starting up bow as well as down bow for further development of your vibrato and tone. ♩ = 60 for all variations.

51. Dolly Died! ♩ = 66 — Wohlfahrt Op. 38, no. 98

52. Largo ♩ = 63 — Handel

53. Santa Lucia ♩ = 100

Neapolitan Boat Song

54. Sunset in Vienna ♩ = 120

Frost

55. Silver Threads Among the Gold ♩ = 69

Hanks

56. The Swan ♩ = 58

Saint-Saëns

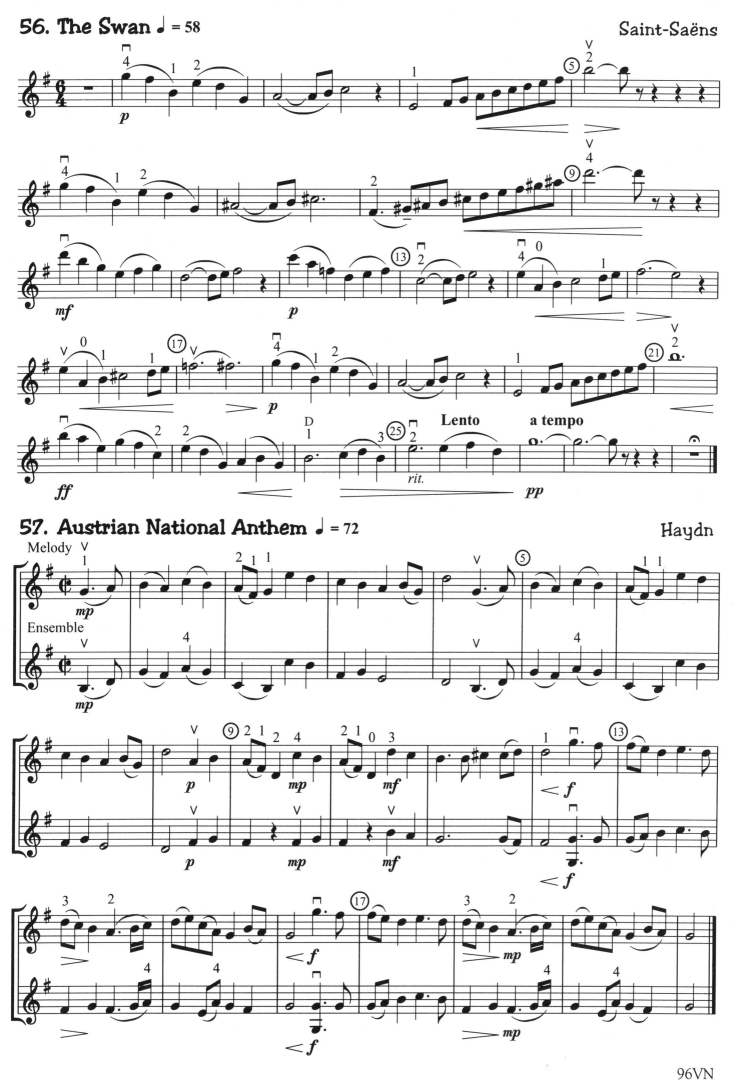

57. Austrian National Anthem ♩ = 72

Haydn

58. Piccolo Caprice ♪ = 108 – 144

Paganini

Learn this piece first at a slower tempo, taking care that all eighth notes, especially ones played by the 4th finger, have vibrato. Move the tempo gradually forward to the faster tempo, making sure that vibrato remains continuous.

59. Intermezzo ♩ = 84

Mascagni

Metronome Acceleration Checklist

This checklist is designed especially for use with the exercises and tunes related to *Swingercise #13*, pages 9–11.

Traditional (keywound) and some electronic metronomes have specific notches for tempo selection. Most digital metronomes have done away with the notch concept entirely, and permit you to select any specific number of beats per minute. Use Checklist A if your metronome is digital. Use Checklist B if you have a metronome which you set mechanically to traditional notches.

Checklist A

☑ Day		Settings		
☐ 1	♪ = 80	85	90	95
☐ 2	♪ = 90	95	100	105
☐ 3	♪ = 100	105	110	115
☐ 4	♪ = 110	115	120	125
☐ 5	♪ = 120	125	130	135
☐ 6	♪ = 130	135	140	145
☐ 7	♪ = 140	145	150	155
☐ 8	♩ = 70	75	80	85
☐ 9	♩ = 80	85	90	95
☐ 10	♩ = 90	95	100	105
☐ 11	♩ = 100	105	110	115
☐ 12	♩ = 110	115	120	125
☐ 13	♩ = 120	125	130	135
☐ 14	♩ = 130	135	140	145
☐ 15	♩ = 135	140	145	150
☐ 16	♩ = 140	145	150	155
☐ 17	♩ = 145	150	160	165
☐ 18	♩ = 150	155	160	165
☐ 19	♩ = 155	160	165	170
☐ 20	♩ = 160	165	170	175
☐ 21	♩ = 165	170	175	180

Checklist B

☑ Day		Settings		
☐ 1	♪ = 80	84	88	92
☐ 2	♪ = 88	92	96	100
☐ 3	♪ = 96	100	104	108
☐ 4	♪ = 104	108	112	116
☐ 5	♪ = 112	116	120	126
☐ 6	♪ = 120	126	132	138
☐ 7	♪ = 132	138	144	152
☐ 8	♩ = 72	76	80	84
☐ 9	♩ = 80	84	88	92
☐ 10	♩ = 88	92	96	100
☐ 11	♩ = 96	100	104	108
☐ 12	♩ = 104	108	112	116
☐ 13	♩ = 112	116	120	126
☐ 14	♩ = 116	120	126	132
☐ 15	♩ = 120	126	132	138
☐ 16	♩ = 126	132	138	144
☐ 17	♩ = 132	138	144	152
☐ 18	♩ = 138	144	152	160
☐ 19	♩ = 144	152	160	168
☐ 20	♩ = 152	160	168	176
☐ 21	♩ = 160	168	176	180

Note: If things seem to be moving too fast, just stay at a comfortable step for a couple of days, or experiment with smaller moves as you advance the metronome (for example, 144–146–148–150 instead of 144–152–160–168). Artistic vibrato speed is attained at about ♩ = 180, or 6 cycles per second. Although vibratos sometimes go as rapidly as 7 ½ cps, it is not very useful, and can be damaging, to push this routine past ♩ =180.

Viva Vibrato! is exciting, innovative, and revolutionary in its approach to teaching vibrato. There has never been anything like it before. Its upbeat style and dialogue, and contemporary design, gently guides students through a five-section curriculum: Vibrato Readiness, The Birth of a Vibrato, The Developing Vibrato, The Maturing Vibrato, The Artistic Vibrato. All teachers of string instruments will find **Viva Vibrato!** user friendly, whether in a private studio or in a homogeneous or heterogeneous string class.

Viva Vibrato! is available for:

Violin   Viola   Cello   String Bass

Piano Accompaniment   Teacher's Manual & Score

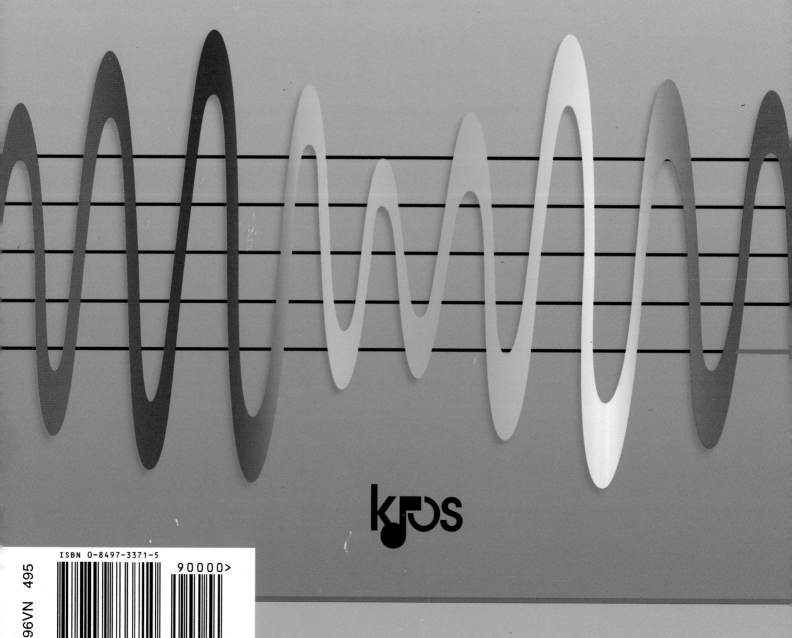

kjos

ISBN 0-8497-3371-5

96VN 495

9 780849 733710

90000>

A workbook for examinations
includes all the scales and arpeggios
for Associated Board exams

Improve
your scales!

VIOLIN

PAUL
HARRIS

FABER *ff* MUSIC